Tarot for Understanding Love and Relationship Patterns

MADE EASY

Tarot for Understanding Love and Relationship Patterns

MADE EASY

Nikki Mackay

Winchester, UK
Washington, USA

First published by Dodona Books, 2012
Dodona Books is an imprint of John Hunt Publishing Ltd., Laurel House, Station Approach,
Alresford, Hants, SO24 9JH, UK
office1@o-books.net
www.o-books.com

For distributor details and how to order please visit the 'Ordering' section on our website.

Text copyright: Nikki Mackay 2011

ISBN: 978 1 78099 093 4

A CIP catalogue record for this book is available from the British Library.

Design: Stuart Davies

Printed and bound by CPI Group (UK) Ltd, Croydon, CR0 4YY
Printed in the USA by Offset Paperback Mfrs, Inc

We operate a distinctive and ethical publishing philosophy in all
areas of our business, from our global network of authors to
production and worldwide distribution.

CONTENTS

Introduction

If you have ever had a tarot reading before you will know that it generally starts off like this:

> "Please take a seat. Now take these cards and shuffle them carefully with your non-dominant hand. Whilst you are shuffling have a think about any areas of your life that you would like to focus on or any questions you might like to ask"

Person shuffles anxiously.

"Okay thank you. I'll just lay the cards out for you. Whilst I'm doing that do you want to tell me if there is an area of your life that you would like me to focus on for you or do you have a question you would like to ask?"

Nine out of ten people consult the tarot for guidance and clarity on a relationship situation. The tenth person does too they just pretend it's about something else...

The tarot is an incredibly powerful tool when it comes to uncovering the ins and outs in relationships. Whether the relationship is of an intimate nature, a family connection or concerns working relationship dynamics the tarot can help to shed light on the hidden truths, the inner thoughts as well as the internal and external pressures on the situation in question.

Wouldn't it be great to see inside your partner's head and figure out how they are really feeling and what they are really thinking? Wouldn't it be helpful to understand why past relationships did not work? Perhaps an understanding of the office politics at play would help to get you up and out of a particular work rut? Maybe looking at a family feud through other family members eyes could bring some healing and calm? The possibilities for exploring the hidden relationship dynamics we encounter on a daily basis are enormous. When you hold a set of Tarot cards in your hand you are holding a key that will unlock the secrets of your relationships. This book will guide you through the complexities and subtleties of the Tarot deck and how to use it specifically to seek understanding and enhance communication in your relationships. So if you would indeed like to know if you are with Mr or Mrs Right or if you would like to be able to move forward from Mr or Mrs Wrong then read on.

2

Brief History of Tarot

The Tarot, best known as a divinatory tool dating from the 15th century, is my first love and continuing passion. I first discovered the Tarot as a teenager and was soon giving readings to friends, parents or friends and teachers. I began to read professionally a couple of years later and the tarot has remained an integral part of my life for 20 years. I am passionate about it, I love working with the tarot and am fascinated with the way in which it can throw light on what appears to be the darkest of situations. If you really want to understand Tarot and work with the cards at any emotional depth then you have to form a relationship with them and learn the language of the Tarot. This connection is unique to each individual and their particular deck. Someone who has spent time looking at each card and noting how the colors, images and depicted scenes makes them feel will be a far better Tarot reader than someone who has learnt a load of traditional meanings by rote. If you can open yourself up to the Tarot and see yourself and your story within it, if you can see the people in your life within the cards, your family, your friends, the people whom you have loved, lost, hated, tolerated or been betrayed by, then you will truly have a deep and clear connection and understanding of the Tarot. If you truly open yourself up to your deck then what is hidden, what is not spoken of, what is confusing to you will then be revealed. You always have a choice about any situation in your life and the Tarot can help to light the path ahead.

Until the last decade or so the history of Tarot has been one that has been pleasantly enshrined in the stuff of legend and myth but now most historians agree that Tarot cards appeared sometime in the mid to late 1400's in Italy, not long after regular playing cards were introduced to Europe in the 14th Century. Generally the Tarot deck consisted of a regular 56-card deck, with a hierarchy of 22 archetypal trump cards. The Tarot underwent a revolution in the early 1900s when occultism and esoteric studies were at the forefront of society again and no discussion on the origins and roots of Tarot would be complete without at least a mention of the Ryder-Waite Deck. Arthur Edward Waite revolutionized the deck with the artist Pamela Coleman-Smith and together they developed pictorial representations of the Minor Arcana suits which until that time had been represented by a series of geometrical patterns and shapes according to the particular suit.

Today the Tarot is widely accepted by many New Age enthusiasts, neo-Pagans, and psychics, as well as those who are interested purely in the study of the cards. The present day interpretation of the Tarot now has some influence from Jungian psychology, early occult and esoteric theory but mainly from AE Waite. There is a huge range of Tarot decks available today, with themes ranging from Celtic myths to Native American and Cat People to Spirals.

When it is used to its full capacity as a spiritual and divinatory system the Tarot can be an amazing tool for enlightenment, transformation and change. Tarot is first and foremost a tool for self-awareness and self-empowerment, allowing observation of yourself, your life, your strengths and those areas causing you difficulty. However this same keen observation can also be applied to those you are connected with, those that you love or have loved allowing you to truly understand the dynamics at play between you.

The Tarot is a gateway to our subconscious, where we store away our hopes and fears, our memories and our true self. All our problems and blockages in life are rooted within our subconscious. By tapping into it, through the use of Tarot, we can find solutions and seek guidance. We can see why the roots of why a relationship has reached stalemate. We can observe the ways in which we maybe communicate differently from the person we are in a relationship with. We can understand their emotional past and take that into account when difficulties arise in the relationship. I have read for so many people who are convinced that their partner is cold and unfeeling and doesn't show any emotion unless a fight is picked and the relationship's future is at stake. When you actually look at it you can see two very different emotionally expressive people, who simply do not communicate in the same way, we all have a line between what is acceptable and what is unacceptable in relationships however we don't all draw that line in the same place.

When you lay out a spread of cards, the unique story of a life appears before you in picture form, with its own individual patterns made up of universal experiences and emotions, a powerful tool for understanding and influencing a life's pattern.

There are traditionally 78 cards in a Tarot deck and within the 78 cards there are 56 Minor Arcana cards and 22 Major Arcana cards. 'Arcana' is the plural of the Latin word, Arcanum, meaning 'secret'. I love that, hidden secrets, secret thoughts, secret hopes and dreams can all be revealed by the Tarot if you know what to look for. Over the years that I have been working with the tarot I have developed my own way of interpreting the cards that follows closely the theories of AE Waite but also encompasses the idea of ancestral knowledge and relationship patterns. It is my personal preference to think of the system of Tarot as having three interlinked aspect of the Major Arcana, the Minor Arcana (encompassing the four suits of Wands, Swords, Cups and Pentacles) and the Court Families of the four suits. No one aspect is more important than another as they are so inter-linked and intertwined. I also like to think of the Tarot in terms of the symbolism of the spiral. A popular teaching method for

Tarot is to lay the entire 78 cards out on a circle, representing the circle of life, working through the Minor Arcana (with Court cards) and then the Major Arcana. This would suggest though that the Tarot (and the journey through life it is representing) comes back to the same point and is static which we know is really not true. I prefer to think in terms of the spiral where once you reach the end of the cycle that you are on, you continue onwards (or regress backwards) on your path taking with you the knowledge and experience as you continue. I also prefer to journey through the Tarot, for teaching and development purposes, starting with the Minor Arcana (through the suits of Wands, Swords, Cups and Pentacles), then in to the transitional and archetypal themes of the 22 cards of the Major Arcana, finishing with the Court Families of the four suits. 78 cards might seem like a lot to learn but you will recognize so many aspects of yourself, your family, your relationships, your experiences and transitions through life that they will soon feel like an extension of you.

3

Choosing Your Tarot Deck

It is essential that you find the right deck for you. Often people feel that they don't connect properly with the Tarot until they have tried several decks, or find that they like one deck for reading, but another for meditation or magic (you may find you end up with quite a collection!) There is a popular myth out there that you have to be gifted your Tarot deck rather than going out and choosing it yourself. In fact it is a much better idea to go out and buy your own, you have to feel a connection to the images within the cards, they must speak to you and you must be comfortable with them. If you really want your deck to be a gift then go out & choose it and then persuade someone else to buy it for you.

Sleep with the deck underneath your pillow, meditate on the cards, start reading with them. Build up that connection as soon as you can. You are learning a new language, a new way of thinking. Feeling completely relaxed and connected to the cards may take time but you can really have fun working towards this point. You have just picked up a key that can open the door into a whole new world.

Tarot works on several different levels, and the most well known is of course fortune telling and divination. To work on this level you just have to know the basic meanings of the cards, a spread to read them by and some confidence to get you started. The more practice you put in, the faster you will gain confidence and find the meanings of the cards become both more familiar and gradually more complex. Through working with Tarot you will also discover intuitive skills you may not even have realized you possessed.

Working on this intuitive level you can begin to view the Tarot as a language and allow your intuitive self to interpret it. When you are reading intuitively you are linking into the unconscious via your psychic abilities. Everybody has psychic ability, and through practice and development, and the right deck, it will become stronger and stronger. Confidence is the key here: you have to believe in yourself and your own abilities and not let the conscious mind get in the way.

Tarot also works on a spiritual level. Through using the Tarot as a tool for guidance on our path we can truly fulfill our potential. Looking deep into the meanings of the cards, and appreciating their significance for our own personal journey can bring us clarity, understanding, and strength, and help us move forward with a clearer sense of purpose.

4

Before We Begin
Enhancing your Natural Psychic Gift

Everyone has a natural 'psychic' or intuitive ability, but we often assume that it is something that only "special people" have or are dismissive of our own intuition. How many times though have you sensed an atmosphere as soon as you walked into a room, or had a strong reaction to someone you have just met? That is your intuition: how many times have you kicked yourself for not listening to it? By listening to it more, tuning in and working with it, it will become stronger and you will trust it more.

Suggestion 1 : Meditation
Choosing a card (daily, weekly or monthly whatever your schedule will allow) to meditate on is another good way both to stimulate your intuitive ability, and gain a deeper connection to the cards. Simply shuffle the cards, holding the intention that whatever card is appropriate for you should come up, and draw one at random from the deck. Spend some time looking at the card, seeing what jumps out at you from it, and sit in meditation to see what message you feel it is bringing you.

Suggestion 2 : Dream work
It is also a good idea to keep a diary of your dreams, if you remember them. They can often provide clues as to what is going on at a deeper level in your personal life, as well as sometimes containing information about the future. Write them down as quickly as possible in the morning, and leave space in your notebook to come back to them at a later time and mark down

anything you can now see was significant in the dream. If you have difficulty remembering your dreams, or if you want to get more out of them, you may want to spend ten minutes meditating before bed, focusing on asking for guidance to come to you in your dreams, and for help in remembering them. It is an excellent practice to meditate on individual tarot cards on a regular basis. Meditation has been used by cultures around the world for thousands of years. The methods and purposes of contemplation vary from Hindu yoga practices, to Buddhist means of spiritual development, to creative visualization techniques and many more.

Common to them is an inner journeying, a voyage to your inner core to discover, integrate and develop your understanding of the various strands of your higher self.

When to meditate

It is best to try to find your own routine for meditation, either early in the morning when you get up or at night before going to bed. If family responsibilities mean that you get little privacy then you will need to think for yourself where and when you can grab 10 - 20 minutes to try to meditate. A regular practice can really help develop your ability to tune in. But even if you only meditate occasionally, it will still have beneficial relaxing effects.

Posture

You don't need to be able to sit in the full lotus position to meditate effectively. Instead you can meditate sitting on a chair, kneeling astride a cushion or stool or sitting cross-legged. You can lie down if you want, but there is a danger of falling asleep.

Don't worry if you do find yourself falling asleep or thinking about your shopping list. You are trying to train the mind to focus and still itself. This won't happen overnight.

Some people experience what's known as "beginner's mind".

This is a sense of clarity and deepness of awareness that they have never had before. This happens because we are so unused to trying to still and integrate the mind that we experience really positive results quite quickly. This might not last! You may have a period where you have great meditation practice, followed by times when it is the hardest thing to do. This is very common, so don't worry about it.

If you have any insights etc during your practice, then take note of them. You could keep a meditation diary.

If after meditating you feel light-headed, dizzy, a bit "spaced out" etc. then you need to ground yourself. Have a cup of tea or water and a snack – sweet things are especially good - to bring you "back into yourself".

If you drift off very easily, then try imagining roots extending from your feet down into the Earth, drawing energy up into your body, keeping you anchored.

5

The Major Arcana

Where the Minor Arcana is concerned with animating everyday life; the Major Arcana deals with traditional archetypes, universal influences and our family roots. These cards shed light on our spiritual and ancestral journey and illustrate turning points in our life, events that will happen or have happened that change our lives. Our attitude to these changes and phases in our life is the key. The situation and changes can work to our advantage or disadvantage depending on our outlook and what we are willing to acknowledge.

I see the Major Arcana as having three distinct aspects or realms (the realm of the family, the ancestors and the dead) within the spiral with the Fool card acting as our guide through each aspect.

The Realm of the Family

The first aspect of the Major Arcana spiral is made up of the first seven numbered cards from The Magician through to the Chariot. It is the aspect that is concerned with who we are in the present situation and the influence our family and relationships are having on us in the immediate moment. It is mainly concerned with personal emotional communication and inter-action with others as we create bonds and forge ties with those around us.

0 – The Fool

The Fool is the naive and innocent child and can be placed anywhere within the Major Arcana as he acts as a guide, think of him as walking you through your relationship patterns. The Fool stands at the start of the journey and represents infinite possibilities and infinite potentials viewing life through the eyes of your inner self, sometimes the inner child. Ready to dive in and be vulnerable once more trusting in love. This card also acts as a bridge over difficult times where a new attitude or a new you needs to emerge. Follow your instinct rather than the rules. In some spreads the Fool is seen with his wand over his shoulder with a knapsack tied around it, this represents your inner power and your experiences in life this far. Good or bad they do not weigh the fool down, they are merely there and part of him. The Fool is normally accompanied by an angel or small animal, this is representative of the inner self/ higher self.

The negative aspect of the fool is naivety, Willful thoughtlessness, an inability to accept life as it truly is, failure to follow your instincts and your heart.

I – The Magician

The High Priestess & the Magician belong together they represent masculine and feminine duality of inner power. The Magician is more representative of being active in the material world the High Priestess is much more passive. This card represents consciousness, action and creation, a very fiery passionate energy. The Magician uses his abilities to manifest things – making something real and tangible from the possibilities represented by the fool. Seize the opportunity to create!
Negative aspects of the Magician is indicated by indecisiveness, misuse of abilities/power. Unwillingness to take control.

2 – The High Priestess

The High Priestess is much more passive. She represents hidden knowledge from the ancestors, intuition and the unconscious mind, the mysteries of life that can only be unlocked through a period of withdrawal. Psychic abilities, hidden wisdom and spirituality are linked to her. She can indicate a need to withdraw and passively assess a potential change/ new beginning. However it can be very tempting to stay withdrawn, and the negative aspect of the High Priestess is associated with this – an extended period of passiveness with a great reluctance to seize the opportunities of life. A balance between the Magician's control and the High Priestess's passivity is needed.

3 – The Empress

The high priestess represents the mental aspect of the female archetype, whereas the empress is motherhood, love and gentleness. Works on a more emotional level with a very passionate approach to life. In a spread the empress represents a period of life where things are approached with passion and high emotions. Can indicate the start of a new project, this is associated with her representation of fertility and growth, she is often portrayed as being pregnant. Negative aspects include a rejection of emotions or desires. Can also indicate acting irrationally.

4 – The Emperor

The empress & emperor represent the male & female archetypes of mother and father. The emperor is an active authoritarian, very masculine, symbolizing power, leadership, ambition and discipline. This card indicates the need for a stable base on which to progress, a need to organize your life & take a more proactive approach to achieving your goals. Be aware of the laws of society in order to see your goal and move towards it. Can also signify a strong, dominating male force in individual's life. Negatively the card can represent obstinacy, hesitancy, stagnation and stifling of passions.

5 – The Hierophant

Also known as the Pope or the High Priest. This card symbolizes traditional values, churches, doctrines and education. Can indicate orthodoxy, conforming to a strict moral path or societies codes of behavior. The emperor represents the rules and the hierophant our obedience. This does not mean there is not room for free thought but perhaps this is not the time for spontaneous action, stick to what you know for a while and then make your judgment. Negatively this card can indicate blind obedience, or a need to rebel for the sake of it.

6 – The Lovers

Relationships, romance, love and sex are all associated with this card. However on a deeper level this card represents choice. Now is the time to make the choice and you must listen to your heart. The card can also represent a need for honest communication. Negatively the card can represent bad choices, temptations & relationship difficulties. This card highlights how we emotionally interact with those around us and how honest we are in our communication.

7 – The Chariot

The chariot indicates great success, over which you have total control. Take control of your life and move forwards, use your will power. Negatively this card can indicate a need to bring a situation under control in a positive way with a view to moving on. You have to take control and make your choice.

The Realm of the Ancestors

The next phase of the Major Arcana is represented by the next seven numbered cards from Strength to Temperance and is the aspect that brings up the patterns from the family generations that influenced your formative years. This aspect really highlights the struggle to come to terms with your place within your family, friendships and relationships.

8 – Strength

A need to confront and release feelings and desires that have been locked away, this is achieved through gentle control of the emotions. Indicates a period of self-development and self-discovery. Being honest with oneself. An ability to face life using inner strength, whatever life throws up.

Negatively can indicate weakness, feeling overwhelmed and pessimistic.

9 – The Hermit

The need for a period of withdrawal to assess the current situation and how you feel about it. The hermit and the lamp he holds represents inner wisdom, inner guidance and knowledge from within. Appears at periods of transition and carries on the theme of self-development from strength. Can also indicate guidance from a teacher/spirit guide.

Negatively the card might indicate that the individual has withdrawn too much from life and now has a fear of returning.

10 – The Wheel of Fortune

This card is based on the ancient belief that our fortunes change in a cyclic manner. The wheel represents the mysteries of fate, also embodies the laws of karma. It signifies a change in circumstance in the individual's life. There may be no obvious reason for this change, however it is the individual's reaction to the change that is key. Do they see it as an opportunity adapt and move on to this new level of their life? Or do they struggle against the change? This card can open your eyes to the responsibility you have to take for your own life.

11 – Justice

Indicates a lesson learned. Look *honestly* at where you are, do you deserve to be here? Did your actions lead to this? When justice appears positively, balance and compensation are indicated. Negatively, it points to a situation that has to be rebalanced fairly. Also associated with legal matters and paperwork.

12 – The Hanged Man
From one angle the hanged man is suspended in space, viewed upside down he is quite happily dancing. Represents independence, being who you are no matter what others think. Can also represent a voluntary sacrifice in order to move on (this is linked to ancient belief systems where self sacrifice was used in order to acquire magical powers such as clairvoyance etc). Negative aspects of this card are indecision or a situation of impossible choice.

13 – Death
This card signifies a time of change, coming to the end of a cycle and a need to let go of what was in order to move on. Death is a positive card if the individual moves with the change and lets go, moving on to new beginnings. Negatively there may be a fear of change and letting go, being stuck in old habits.

14 – Temperance
The word 'temperance' is derived from the Latin word 'temperare' which means 'to mix' or 'combine properly'. This card represents the ability to combine all parts of the self to be true and accepting of who you really are. In a reading this card shows a need for patience, balance and timing. Can indicate that the best thing to do at this time is nothing. Negatively this card can indicate extremes of actions or personalities.

The Realm of the Dead
The final aspect of the Major Arcana uncovers some of the deeper relationship patterns that have been passed down through the generations as well as experienced through our own personal relationships that become an inherent part of who we are. It can

be more difficult to release and clear the energy associated with this aspect of the Major Arcana as the patterns are often old or entrenched. The ancestral energy that is influent from the Realm of the Dead is from those ancestors that are not at peace, who have been excluded or who have not been acknowledged. Of course those that we refuse to let go of and be at peace in a relationship sense also have significant influence here, both in the symbolic world of the Tarot as well as our own reality. It is represented by the final seven numerical cards of the Major Arcana, from the Devil through to the World.

The quests started in the family and ancestral realms of the Major Arcana can often involve intense but one-sided relationships with other individuals that are similarly disconnected from their family, this is highlighted by the ancestral aspect of the cycle in particular with The Devil and The Tower. The Devil especially highlights the self-destructive patterns of addictive behaviors such as alcoholism, drug and even food addiction. These addictions again link back to the rejection of the family and relationship influences of the Empress and the Emperor and reflect the communication issues of the Lovers although the patterns held may be older than the current or previous relationship in question.

15 – The Devil

The Devil links back to the lovers with the theme of choices and shows an individual feeling trapped in a situation but unwilling to make the choice to change. The card can also indicate that the individual is letting their desires overpower their judgment and that they are not basing their decisions on the full facts. There is a need here to break free from a negative situation or negative behavior pattern that really belongs to another. Again as mentioned previously the theme of the Devil is strongly linked to addictions and substance abuse. There can be interesting links to the Emperor and the Hierophant. The link to the Lovers and emotional communication can result in very destructive relationship patterns for women.

16 – The Tower

The Tower represents difficult experiences and violent upheaval that can be repeated throughout relationships if not addressed properly. Situations or states of mind that have outlived their usefulness are about to be destroyed to make way for new growth. This process is painful if the individual doesn't accept the need for change. The initial sharp shock ultimately leads to freedom and new beginnings.

17 – The Star

Peace, healing and recovery after the emotional trauma of the tower. This card represents hope, a sense of wholeness and healing of the inner and outer self. The future is looking bright. Negatively this card can indicate an unwillingness to move on.

18 – The Moon

A card that represents the imagination. The moon reflects the hidden light from the sun. A time to let go of logic and to follow the intuition. The unconscious is being stimulated and is stirring. At this time the individual may begin to experience strange emotions, dreams and fears. Listen to and trust yourself. Do not be influenced by others. May indicate a period of withdrawal with the purpose of accepting who and where you are. Negatively can indicate someone who is easily led or deceived by others.

19 – The Sun

Freedom, letting go, breaking loose, liberation, joy and happiness! After the night comes the dawn and this card represents all things good in life. Success is strongly indicated, a time for optimism, energy and wonder. Also indicates support from others on your journey. Negatively the individual may not quite see where they are going in life.

20 – Judgment

It is time to grab the bull by the horns and make the change. The individual is surrounded by opportunity. Let go and accept the past and move on with your new life. Individual has to be proactive in this, they will be stuck where they are if they do not work for the change. This card is also associated with Karmic balance, you will reap what you have sown, so act responsibly. Negatively this card indicates a hesitation.

21 – The World

Completion and unity. Journey's end and on to new beginnings. Your plans have succeeded, you are self aware, life is harmonious and balanced. Pause, enjoy what you have accomplished, then continue the dance of life.

Negative aspects indicate blocked energies.

6

The Minor Arcana

On the surface, the Minor Arcana may appear to deal with mundane everyday issues but scratch the surface and they are a gateway to your psychological, spiritual and physical realities. They offer guidance on our chosen path, showing us the patterns at play within our lives and point towards their origin, mapping out the entanglements. They animate the patterns and allow them to come to life.

The Minor Arcana is made up of the four suits of wands, cups, swords and pentacles, each containing 10 number cards. In many traditional decks (pre Rider-Waite) the minor Arcana or "pip" cards as they were known, numbers 1-10 of the four suits were simply illustrated with geometric shapes representing their suit, much like playing cards. However the deck designed by Arthur Edward Waite and the artist Pamela Coleman-Smith in 1910 revolutionized this and most decks that have been published since then base the minor Arcana on the Rider-Waite version with an illustration on each card. Whereas the Major Arcana depict traditional archetypes, the Minor Arcana show scenes and depictions from everyday life. They animate the experiences, transitions, communications and challenges that we go through in our life and by getting to know them we can recognize aspects of ourselves and those around us within them. The numbered cards from 1 to 10 show the journey through a particular aspect of the minor Arcana, the difficulties, successes, and experiences are altered by the suit. For example the journey through the suit of swords is very different to the journey through the suit of cups. An individual whose personal emotional experiences are rooted mainly in the watery cups will communicate very differently and have different expectations to someone who resonates more with the fiery wands. Of course life is never that simple that we will all have a single affiliation to one particular suit but you can begin to see how a person's previous emotional baggage may be carried forward and imprinted on future relationships. If two people don't share a similar emotional 'root' then they will find it difficult to 'see' one another as we tend to view people how we would like to see them according to our own emotional understanding rather than as they actually are.

The Four Suits

The suit of Wands relates to the element of fire, to spiritual willpower, to inspiration, to passion, action and creation. There is a lot of movement and energy in the wands and the people within the cards react strongly to whatever situation they find themselves in and are either fired up and raring to go or burned out and burdened. In interesting aspect of the wand suit is to teach us how to direct the fire of our inspiration in ourselves and in our lives, how to harness the fire within as a positive inner force for change.

The suit of cups is related to the element of water. They are concerned with dreams, feelings, romantic love and healing. The people within the suit of cups have a soft dreamlike quality about them that can be very attractive to others initially but they are not always based in reality. Intuition is strongly associated with the cups and people who resonate with the cups can be very strongly in tune with themselves and those around them, however if they are denying some aspect of themselves or have drifted off their path then the lack of logic and reality can be particularly difficult and irritating to deal with.

The suit of swords relate to the element of air. Swords have the reputation, unjustifiably of being very negative. They can signify pain, anger and destruction, but more importantly they are associated with the realm of mental ability, ideas, communication and leadership. They appear when there is a need to cut through illusions and complicated problems in life. This is their main function, to show us how to clear away blocks so we can move on and heal. Those who resonate with swords have often had difficult emotional experiences be it in childhood with their family or within their intimate relationships and can find it challenging to open themselves up emotionally. There are those within the suit though who have worked through this and go on to help others either in a formal counseling capacity as part of their work or informally in the friendships and relationships they form.

The suit of pentacles is concerned with the physical world and the magic and wonder present around us every day. This suit covers everything from work, money, business, physical pleasure, health and security. Don't fall into the trap of just associating pentacles with money, this suit goes much deeper than that. Those who link strongly with the suit can often be thought of a dull or withdrawn by those who don't really know them but they do say it is the quiet ones that you have to look out for and if you take the time to get to know them you will be amazed at what lurks underneath the surface. They are by nature incredibly stubborn and will doggedly stick to a path through to ultimate success or failure once they have decided something.

Let's have a bit of a closer look...

The Suit of Cups

The Ace of Cups

The ace of cups is a lovely, positive card. A new beginning and fresh start in the realm of love. It heralds an injection of energy and movement, a new start in love. Often a time of happiness, joy and love. Can be a very intense period where all other thoughts and projects are placed on hold and the new love interest is given top priority. If a card could epitomize falling head over heels in love and feeling like a teenager then this is that card.

The Two of Cups

This is the beginning of a new relationships, the coming together of two people. Not necessarily always a romantic partnership, this card can also signify a working relationship or business partnership but it will be a working relationship with a significant emotional investment. It shows too people coming together as equals whether it remains that way will be indicated by the other cards surrounding it in the tarot spread.

The Three of cups

This card often indicates a shared joy. A time of celebration and happiness and togetherness. Sharing and being surrounded by loved ones. Can signify a happy family event such as a birth , marriage, or the growth of an established relationship. In business terms it would signify a success end to a project or a promotion.

The Four of Cups

In stable emotional situation but feeling thoroughly disenchanted. The stability can become stagnation if we don't move forward from the solid base that has been created. Can suggest that an individual is re-evaluating their relationship (romantic or business) or that the novelty has worn off. A sense of dissatisfaction with personal relationships, feeling stuck in an emotional rut, but not noticing new developments that are right under their nose.

The Five of Cups

The Scottish word scunnered sums this one up (Scots word

meaning to be disgusted, bored or simply fed up). Disappointment. Confusion. Loss. Disappointment and with another's behavior and frustration that the time and emotional investment made is stagnating. There is a need to honestly look at the situation and see where your responsibility lies and to let the rest go. This card will often come up when someone is repeating a relationship pattern either the same partner behaving in the same way again and again or with a series of partners that all turn out to have similar traits.

The Six of cups
Aaaahh a sigh of relief. A card of positive change, success and recovery. An end to the negative energies of the five of cups. This card often indicates the recovery of a relationship either a couple coming through a difficult time together or a relationship rekindling after a period of separation. There is a softness and understanding of the other person with this card, an acceptance of things being just as they are.

The Seven of Cups
Illusion and deceit are often indicated with the seven of cups either deceitfulness in others or a refusal to face the facts about someone else's behavior. Whatever the case a wake up call to find the truth in the situation and not accept things at face value. Dig a little deeper. In working relationships it is telling you that you do not have all the facts, people around you are possibly misleading you. Try to take a logical approach with your head and not your heart.

The Eight of Cups
This card is closely linked to the four of cups. If the stagnation felt there isn't addressed this is often the next stage of deterioration. There is a need for change and if it is not acted upon this will lead to feelings of stifling and further stagnation. It can

show boredom and lack of interaction in a relationship (business and personal). There is often a feeling that there is something missing or hidden, although on the outside, to others, everything looks okay.

The Nine of Cups

This is a very positive card and indicates happiness and success in what you choose to pour your energy into. This card is also known as the wish card and joy and fulfillment and there for you. It is a matured version of the ace of cups showing someone who has worked with that initial surge of positive and overwhelming emotion and turned it into something real and tangible.

The Ten of Cups

This card instills a real sense of 'place' on an individual level and a sense of peace and acceptance for those around you. It is the end of a cycle and the cycle has ended with a sense of fulfillment and completion. A very stable and happy base, this happy situation will not end in the near future it will evolve and grow naturally.

The Suit of Swords

The Ace of Swords

A new beginning and a fresh start on an intellectual level. A meeting of minds. A breath of fresh air. A time for action and putting new ideas in to practice. Success is shown in a new venture or intellectually stimulating pursuit with an opportunity waiting to be grasped. Can also show new understanding about an emotional entanglement, the penny finally dropping on the 'why me?' of a situation and the freedom to cut the binds that tie and to move on.

The Two of Swords

This card indicates difficult choices and a struggle to keep things on an even keel for those around you. This card often comes up when you have been trying to do the right things for others and have lost your sense of self in the process. You can't stay in this situation forever, a choice has to be made and others have to learn to compromise and take responsibility for themselves. Listen to your emotions - don't shut them off, you already know what you need to do.

The Three of Swords

This can be a difficult one as the energies of the previous card, the two of swords, starts to gain momentum and flow. The realization that you have to walk away from something or someone that you care about is very hard to bear. Yet you cannot save them, the responsibility for their fate lies with them. By staying you are sacrificing part of who you are and shutting out opportunities for change for yourself. A need for acceptance of the situation before moving on and letting go.

The Four of Swords

A strong sense of passivity and peace. A withdrawal to reconsider a situation, and to rest and regain strength. Isolation. The need to seek guidance, either from others or your own higher self. Be very gentle with yourself (or the individual represented by this card). It may seem like slipping away but things will return to a more stable footing.

The Five of Swords

Ouch. Upheavals, blocks, restrictions and disappointment are generally indicated by this card. A situation that has gotten a little bit out of control with everyone reacting in an aggressive way and forgetting why they feel so strongly in the first place. Defeat and loss for all concerned if the situation is allowed to continue, try to detach as no-one is listening to sense at the moment. Take stock and see if this really if your fight or if perhaps retreat is the best option here.

The Six of Swords
Thank goodness, an end to the negative energies of five. A positive card of healing and change. A recovery of a situation is indicated with a quiet passage through a difficult time. The emotional scars will remain but the memories will fade. You are ready now to move on.

The Seven of Swords
This card often comes up when someone you are involved with is being less than honest. Check carefully to see that you have the truth about your working and emotional life, if you have a sneaking suspicion that something isn't quite right then investigate. Don't rush in feet first though, check things thoroughly and carefully before you confront anyone and be very careful about who you trust. When this card comes up in a reading representing a situation from the past it is showing you that you haven't quite dealt with a betrayal. Let it go or be prepared to carry it into all your future relationships.

The Eight of Swords
This card shows indecision and a reluctance to see the situation as it really is. Oppression and feeling trapped. Feeling insecure and in an apparently inescapable problem. In truth nothing prevents you from leaving this situation but yourself. Sometimes it is easier to be a martyr than to be the one responsible for changing a situation or ending a relationship. Open your eyes and take a good look around you.

The Nine of Swords
The world is weighing heavily on your shoulders and there is

sorrow and mental anguish. This card can come up and refer to a situation happening to someone close rather than the person being read for directly. There is great fear of speaking about the situation, a sense that things have to be secret and unseen which heightens the sense of isolation and shame. This card can also indicate someone who is unconsciously carrying a burden of guilt for another's actions.

The Ten of Swords
Well the good news is that it can't get any worse than this, welcome to emotional rock bottomness and betrayal. Things are as bad as they could possibly be, but they are about to get better. There is a light at the end of the tunnel and the worst is over. You are a survivor and don't you forget it.

The Suit of Wands

The Ace of Wands
This is an injection of creative, fiery energy and movement, a new start. When you see this card you see the spark coming back in to someone's eyes, a reigniting of the spirit within and the energy to simply "go for it" and achieve goals. It can also herald the beginning of a very passionate and physical love affair.

The Two of Wands
Plans being made, choices weighed up and opportunities to decide upon. There really is a need to move onwards and upwards whilst still being mindful of your responsibilities. This card can indicate an uprooting of where you are based and a period of travel or temporary relocation for love or work. Go with it.

The Three of Wands
Can you do it? Yes you can! Things really are looking up and

change is coming. Plans are being made, opportunity is in abundance and the prospects are good. Much is still unknown to you at this time and you may need to leave your comfort zone both emotionally and physically but if you do you will end up with what you have always wanted deep down. The change will be worth it.

The Four of Wands

This bodes well for your relationship. There is a strong sense of completion of one phase and committing to the next. Order and stability in the home life. Sowing the seeds for the future. Marriage or a deepening of the level of commitment within a relationship is indicated. Enjoy.

The Five of Wands

Things are restricted just now and communication is difficult and misconstrued. Check in and make sure that you are not fighting & arguing for the sake of it. Who are you really angry with? It doesn't feel like it is the person bearing the brunt of your frustrations. Use your energy in a more positive way.

The Six of Wands

Thankfully an end to a negative cycle of events and you have come out on top. Do you really need more encouragement to believe in yourself and your abilities? Go for it, you will succeed. There is a sense of coming home, being appreciated by others and a relationship getting back on track.

The Seven of Wands

You really need to stand up for yourself and what you believe in. This is a challenge and won't necessarily be easy to make the other person see your point of view but you need to embrace it to rise out of the rut you are in.

The Eight of Wands

Lots and lots of movement, things changing around you very quickly. A time of swift action and change. Travel or a house move may be indicated. A real feeling of being swept off your feet, even though you might not feel in control you are safe.

The Nine of Wands

You need to find your inner strength just now. You might feel hemmed in and surrounded by conflict but you need to resist fighting, there is another way and you voice will be heard. Wait until you have all the facts in front of you so that you can understand the 'why' of the situation before you react.

The Ten of Wands

Let's be honest this is not a good situation to be in and you probably have been here before. You need to extract yourself from your emotional ties and put yourself first. You are weighed down by commitments, a need to be free. You are only burdened down by your own actions though and you do have the power to free yourself, unfortunately you can't make it better for everyone else at the same time.

The Suit of Pentacles

The Ace of Pentacles

Woohoo! A new beginning in your world most likely a fresh start in your working life or the opportunity to turn a dream in to a reality. This is a really prosperous time for you as others are really seeing you for who you truly are. You can begin again.

The Two of Pentacles

The grass isn't always greener on the other side you know. Change for the sake of change is never really worth it. Look instead at what is making you feel unsettled and do something about that rather than giving in and running away. Try and go with the flow for a bit and see what comes up within you.

The Three of Pentacles

Haven't you done well! An acknowledgement of you and your unique skills and talents. This card shows a recognition of hard work and perseverance. A step up both emotionally and materially. Emotional and mental growth resulting in material benefits.

The Four of Pentacles

This card shows someone who is feeling cornered and boxed in. Uncertainty about who to trust or let in. Someone who is emotionally closed off and feeling fearful. Now is not the time to attempt a heart to heart. They need to take responsibility for your own actions, and have a little faith in the universe.

The Five of Pentacles

A feeling of insecurity is dominant here. Also a feeling of being excluded from something or shut out. If in a relationship the partners previous relationships have not been dealt with cleanly, a strong sense of overlap. There has been a breakdown of communication and this needs to be reopened quickly in order for all concerned to feel they have a place.

The Six of Pentacles

A coming together of people who were previously at odds with one another, a new level of understanding and sharing is achieved. Generosity of spirit and compassion for others should be welcomed and seen for what it is. There is no place for jealousy here.

The Seven of Pentacles

Things are feeling a little bit blocked and if the door isn't opening for you perhaps it is because you are knocking on the wrong door. Plans not working out as fast as you expect. Try not to become frustrated, be patient and look and see the effect on those around you. It isn't all about you.

The Eight of Pentacles

Your hard work and patience is definitely paying off. You have taken control of your own destiny and future and it is really paying off. It may not have been the easiest of paths to pick but you have made it. Well done.

The Nine of Pentacles

Success and good fortune seem to be in abundance all around you and people looking at you and your life would assume that you were really 'living the dream' however there is an emotional restlessness about you. You need to address what is going on inside your heart and what it is you really want in your life, it isn't too late to make a change.

The Ten of Pentacles

This is a very positive place to be. There is a strong sense of emotional security in your relationship and you truly love your partner and they love you. Settled family life, in an established happy home. Security. This shouldn't be taken for granted, be aware of your blessings.

7

The Court Families

This brings us on to the Court Families. In my opinion the Court Families are the people that have journeyed through the spiral of life and have the scars to prove it. They carry with them the knowledge of the element of their particular suit as well as the archetypal knowledge of the Majòr Arcana that they have journeyed through. They represent you, your family members and your ancestors and when you connect to them they become you, your family members and ancestors and tell the tales of your life, your family life and the patterns therein. They can show you how these patterns are being acted out by the people surrounding you and the different situations occurring in your life.

The four suits of the Minor Arcana (Wands, Swords, Cups and Pentacles) all have elemental associations which represent the essence of the suit and its purpose.

We start with the suit of Pentacles. It is concerned with the physical world, our family line, our relationship and our place in it. The function of this suit is to help us to ground ourselves in order to progress and literally "find our feet" in who we are and where we come from.

We then move on to the suit of swords which is the element of air. Swords have the reputation, unjustifiably of being very negative. They can signify pain, anger and destruction however being the element of air is very often the perception of something rather than a physical reality. They signify a need to cut through illusion and pain. Their main function is to give clarity on where we are in the present moment, to show us any patterns or blocks and what needs to be done to clear them so we can move on and heal. So, in essence they highlight the burdens or fates from the previous relationships that we are carrying forward.

Next is the suit of cups. Cups are related to the element of water which is concerned with emotion and emotional communication, connections with others and our intuitive sense of self. The Cups indicate and suggest where the healing of the past karma from old relationships needs to occur.

The suit of Wands relates to the element of fire, which embodies connection to spirit, transformation, change, clearing, and the drive to move forward.

Below is a guide to the Court Families, with their masculine and feminine aspects. The feminine line is carried by the Page (Princess in some decks) and the Queen; the masculine line is carried by the Knight and the King.

The Wand Family

The Wand Family helps us to understand where we are being blocked, where change needs to occur and what needs to be cleared through their element of Fire with strong male energy.

The Female Line

The Page

The female line of the Wand family in youth is not rooted in who she is; there is a need to look to previous relationships and her connection to family in order to help her find her place. She quickly loses interest and moves on amassing a pile of unfinished tasks and relationships.

The Queen

The older female Wand, with the patterns left unchecked, will have amassed many responsibilities through her inability to say no to her passions. She is open to emotional blackmail and her interaction with the male line is often destructive upon her, she is ruled by her passion and guilt. It would be wise to look to the former partners of this lady to see the path that lies behind her.

The Male Line

The Knight

The young male Wand has an unquenchable desire to prove himself to family and those close to him often losing sight of why he has started something. He seeks to be seen and is often overlooked.

The King

As he grows older he becomes strong minded, dominating and assertive and often appears as a 'block' for individuals to overcome as he has little awareness of others on their own path as he expects everyone else to follow him to the fates that he himself is bound to follow.

The Sword Family

The Sword family brings us the honest clarity of where we are in the present and what influences or patterns from the past are affecting us in the present. They show us, in their own particular style, what we need to cut from our lives or what thought patterns we need to release. There is strong female energy with the Swords.

The Female Line

The Page

The young female Sword is hesitant to put herself back out there and have the same pattern repeat itself (this can be a perception rather than a learned behavior as she strongly carries the experiences that she grew up with). Guarded and detached in emotional relationships and communication, she can seem cold to outsiders.

The Queen
The sense of detachment continues as she grows older, she is excellent at seeing others as they really other but cannot apply this emotional logic to herself. She feels isolated from her masculine counterparts.

The Male Line

The Knight
In youth he is completely reactionary. Everything is in his head and is intellectualized and he finds emotional communication uncomfortable. He is constantly on the defensive as he is not rooted in who he is, he feels trapped between doing what he should do and doing what he wants to do.

The King
With age he becomes calm, calculating with a tendency for narrow-mindedness. He 'remembers' the pains from past relationship hurts and carries them with him unconsciously which leads him to detach. He finds emotional communication difficult and feels disconnected from the influence women in his life. He often has a string of broken relationships behind him to match with the Queen of Wands. His detachment leads him to feel little for others though he can appear very charming.

The Cup Family
The Cup Family carries the knowledge of how and where to heal Karma from the past and has a strong female influence.

The Female line

The Page
In youth the female cup is ruled by her emotions and intuition and holds on to other people's emotions like a sponge. She has the energy of being stuck between different loyalties (previous partners, friends etc) but feels extreme loyalty her female friends as there is often a pattern of trauma relationships for her and those she chooses to have in her life.

The Queen
As she ages is still ruled by emotion but instead of focusing on her own emotions (like the page) she finds it more comfortable to work with other people's emotions in order to move them forward, staying firmly stuck herself. She has an intuitive knowledge of past relationship mistakes for others but refuses to acknowledge or clear her own. Here you will find many a social worker, carer or therapist unconsciously trying to free themselves by helping others.

Male Line

The Knight
So obsessed is the young male with his own emotions and his own perfection that he is oblivious to others. Is constantly trying to live up to an ideal that he has set for himself that simply isn't achievable.

The King
He grows up with far more awareness and guilt. He is more comfortable in feminine company and feels unexplained guilt because of this; he will put family and responsibility to family before himself and is often mistreated within this role.

The Pentacle Family

The Pentacle family brings the karmic influences from previous relationships in to our physical reality as well as carrying a strong male energy.

The Female Line

The Page

She is overly influenced by what is expected of her and has a tendency to veer towards men and doesn't receive the respect of women in her life. She will shoulder the responsibility for old guilt and needs to release it.

The Queen

As she matures she can often find herself placed in a role as she carries forward the responsibilities that belong to others. She is the grown up version of the young page that hasn't realized that she is living her life for someone else. Often the Father will be her ideal man and no one else will match up to him in her eyes.

The Male Line

The Knight

In youth he is someone who sticks to his path as he sees it and will take the road that is right for him even if it is the road less travelled. He is determined, strong willed and sticks to his guns. He is unconsciously finishing what those before him have started and has a stronger family link with the older generations rather than his peers.

The King

He becomes a self made man from the school of hard knocks who strives to be a provider so that the past does not catch up with him. He often has no awareness of why he strives so hard and can lose sight of a relationship or his family as he is driven by the past. Releasing the past will free him from this, there is a positive relationship with the Mother but the Father is often detached (e.g. masculine line of the Sword family).

The Court Cards can often be the most difficult to interpret in a tarot spread. Traditionally they are meant to refer to people surrounding the individual but they can also appear to describe situations. They can appear as significators (highlighting the theme of the reading), they can represent you or the individual you are reading for; they can act as modifiers, commenting on the situation; as agents, people in the individual's life who are influencing the situation; or they can act in the same way as the other Minor Arcana cards, highlighting a situation, event or emotional issue in the individual's life. There are no rules about deciding which category the court cards fall in to in the spread, its meaning should usually be clear from its position within the spread and the surrounding cards. However, if in doubt focus on the card as a personality, this is the most likely significance. The simplest way to get to grips with the court cards is to get to know them and who they represent in your circle or family, friends or partners.

Accessing the energy of the Tarot through a visualization meditation is a very effective way of linking in and getting to know the court families. If you have a Tarot deck that you currently work with you may want to lay out the four Court Families and spend some time familiarizing yourself with them for the next exercise. It would be useful to either read through the exercise a few times before you try it, to record it (leaving sufficient space for your own personal exploration) or to have a friend read it aloud for you. The family members that come to you during the exercise may be people known to you or they may be symbolic representations.

Exercise for Connection to your own Court Families

It's probably best to be lying down for this meditation, make sure that you are comfortable and warm before you start. You may need a blanket as your body temperature may drop when you are relaxed.

Close your eyes and relax down your body. Imagine water flowing over the front of your body washing away any tension or stress from your face your neck and chest, your legs, all washed away through the soles of your feet into the earth. Now imagine water flowing down over the back of your body, washing any tension and stress from the back of your head, your neck, your shoulders, back and legs. All this is washed into the earth through the soles of your feet. Now imagine water flowing through your crown chakra, flowing through your entire body, cleansing you of any stressful thoughts or emotions, taking away any stress and tension, all this flowing away through the soles of your feet leaving you completely relaxed.

Now visualize yourself lying down in the middle of a clearing. You are lying down on a blanket; the sun is shining and warming you. There is a light breeze ruffling the grass and trees surrounding your clearing. You are completely at peace.

Now it is time to invite in the Fool from the Major Arcana. He is going to be your guide for this journey. Notice how he looks, how he makes you feel. Spend some time connecting with his energy and listen to what he has to say.

Once you have connected with the Fool it is time to ask him to bring to you the members of the wand family who bring the element of Fire. Notice how they look, how they makes you feel. Spend some time connecting with their energy and listen to what they have to say. When you are ready ask them "What is my fear?" listen and feel the message they bring to you. Thank them and allow them to leave.

It is now time to ask the Fool to bring to you the members of the Sword family who bring the element of Air. Notice how they look, how they makes you feel. Spend some time connecting with their energy and listen to what they have to say. When you are ready ask them "What do I need to release and let go of?" Listen and feel the message they bring to you. Thank them and allow them to leave.

It is now time to ask the Fool to bring to you the members of the Cup family who bring the element of Water. Notice how they look, how they makes you feel. Spend some time connecting with their energy and listen to what they have to say. When you are ready ask them "What do I need to heal?" listen and feel the message they bring to you. When you feel ready thank them and allow them to move onwards.

It is now time to ask the Fool to bring to you the members of the Pentacle family forward who bring the element of Earth. Again notice how they look, how they makes you feel. Spend some time connecting with their energy and listen to what they have to say. When you are ready ask them "What is my purpose?" listen and feel the message they bring to you. Thank them and allow them to leave.

Spend some time again alone with the Fool, you can ask him if he has any further guidance for you. When you are ready gradually bring your awareness back to the room you are sitting in, become more aware of your physical body, wriggle your fingers and toes. When you are ready open up your eyes.

You may want to spend some time recording your experience so that you do not forget it, what seems vivid and unforgettable at the time does have a tendency to slip away and you will be doing further work with this experience.

8

Tarot Spreads

After you have been working with tarot for a while and are comfortable with the cards you may not feel it necessary to use a tarot spread, you will just be able to lay out a few cards and intuitively receive the meanings. Until then a spread will help you find the meaning of your reading. After the cards have been shuffled (by you if you are reading for yourself or by the individual in question if you are reading for someone else) you will lay out the cards from the top of the pile onto specific positions, each position in a spread has its own significance. The meanings of the cards, the position within the spread and your own intuition are then used to interpret the reading. It is important to interpret the spread as a whole, looking at the patterns within, rather than going along and interpreting on a card by card basis. The reading flows much better this way. Many spreads have a card called the "significator". This card is picked out first by the individual after the initial shuffle, the deck is then handed back to them and they shuffle again. The significator can be seen to represent the individual or can act as an overall "theme" card for the reading. There are many different types of spread, the following are a few examples. I will also go on to discuss designing your own spread.

The secret to becoming a good tarot reader is practice, practice and more practice. Read for yourself, read for friends, read for as many different people as you can in the beginning. It can feel quite daunting to read for someone you don't know but soon it will become your preference! It can be tempting to just to conclusions when reading for a friend or to fall in to the trap of telling them what you would like to happen rather than what you are actually seeing in the cards. Reading for someone you don't know is much easier, you have no preconceived ideas so simply just get on with the reading itself. Many years ago now I worked for a year or so on a psychic phone line and I enjoyed being able to link in and focus purely on the connection and the reading itself rather than having the distraction of someone sitting in front of me! If you really can't find someone to practice on or you just don't feel confident about it then a good tip is to start to read the agony columns and problem pages in magazines. Then do a reading for the person who is asking the question, if you do this try and speak aloud to the person as if they were in front of you that way you will focus more on the flow of the reading as you are speaking your thoughts aloud.

Before you begin your reading you should ask for protection and guidance, I call on the help of the angels of Tarot and divination. You can say a prayer, ask for help from a guide or visualize yourself surrounded by white light, whatever feels most comfortable. Shuffle the cards before you pass them over to your individual, my preference is to shuffle with the non-dominant hand as the intuitive side of your brain controls this hand. Next pass the cards to your individual and ask them to shuffle in the same way whilst thinking about what they would like to know. It is a good idea to try and get your individual to focus on their question and also to relate that question, or at least the area it concerns, to you. People may be unwilling to tell you why they want a reading saying "you're psychic, you should know". This can be equated to going to a Doctor and saying "I'm not feeling well, you are a doctor you should be able to know why & make me better". If they tell you why they want a reading and share their hope/fear then you will be able to give them a greater insight than if you are just giving a general reading. Don't be afraid to ask the individual what their question is! They should shuffle for as long as they feel the need to. Next the individual should pick the significator, I like to spread the cards on the table face down for them to choose. Get them to shuffle again and hand the cards back to you. It is now time to lay the spread. Once you have laid out the spread take a deep breath and centre yourself before you say anything, have a good look at the spread, see what jumps out at you straight away. Is there an obvious theme, a dominance of one suit or a lot of Major Arcana cards? Once you have done that start your reading with confidence.

The Three Card Spread

Figure 1 - The Three Card Spread

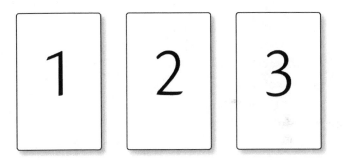

1 – Past influences
2 – Present situation
3 – Final outcome (future)

This is a very simple spread to begin using. The spread can be expanded upon by adding clarification cards onto the original three cards. If 3 is a negative card a 4th card can be added to show how the situation can be dealt with or to take it to a comfortable point of resolution. You can set out a three card spread for both parties in a relationship to contrast and compare how they are both feeling.

Sample Spread

Figure 2 - Sample Three Card Spread

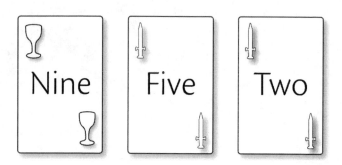

Question: Is there anything left between me and my ex.
1 The Nine of Cups
2 The Five of Swords
3 The Two of Swords

Interpretation

Well the short answer here would be no. If you notice the simple progression from the watery, emotional cups in the past position that flows into the realm of the suit of swords with the present and future which holds the energy of thoughts, fears and things that need to be released or cut from our lives you can understand my short answer! To look in a little more depth the nine of cups in the past position tells us that perhaps the client is looking back at the relationship through rose tinted glasses or maybe just remembering the initial high that comes in at the start of a whirlwind romance. The five of swords flowing into the 2 of swords tells us that there are difficulties in the relationship, particularly around communication and that if the client were to go back and reignite a relationship with this person then they would likely be compromising who they were and have to sacrifice their own hopes and dreams in the process.

. What would be useful here would be to expand this spread and explore whether this type of relationship is a common occurrence for the client and if they are attracted to partners that they feel the need to save or rescue to avoid looking at what is really going on for themselves. The next spread we will discuss would be perfect!

The Celtic Cross Spread

This is perhaps the most famous of the Tarot spreads and is widely used. There are various different versions of the spread, the one I shall give you has 11 cards which I find useful, other versions have only 10 cards.

Figure 3 - The Celtic Cross Spread

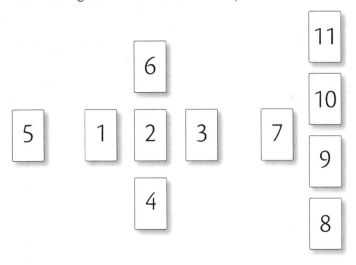

1 – The significator. Represents the individual and the influences surrounding them at the moment.

2 – The Present. Immediate influences on the situation.

3 – The crossing card. Negative or blocking energies on the situation. If it is a positive card it shows the strength/

qualities that are needed to overcome the situation.

Cards 1, 2 & 3 should be read together as a "snapshot" of the individual's current situation.

4 – Deep past. Past energies that are affecting the current situation. Not necessarily a long time into the past but deeply affecting.

5 – The recent past. More recent energies affecting the situation.

Cards 4, 5 & 7 should be read together to see how the past is influencing the future.

6 – The goal. What the individual hopes to achieve or obtain.

7 – The immediate future. The short term outcome. If negative it may indicate something the individual needs to deal with before they can move on.

8 – Personal influences. The individual's feeling on the situation.

9 – External influences. How others view and influence the situation.

10 – Hopes and fears.

11– The final outcome. What will happen based on the influences surrounding the individual at the time.

Cards 6, 7, 10 & 11 will give a full explanation of the final outcome and how to get there.

When I lay out a Celtic cross, I mutter it all to myself: 'This is you (1), This is your situation (2), this crosses you (3), this lies below you (4), this lies behind you (5), this lies above you (6), this lies in front of you (7), what you bring, what others bring, hopes & fears, where you're heading' – I like the below-behind-above-in front bit: it fixes why the cards are placed in those positions

Figure 4 - Sample Celtic Cross Spread

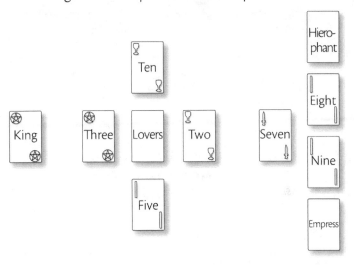

Question: Does our relationship have a future?

1   **The Three of Pentacles**
2   **The Lovers**
3   **The Two of Cups**
4   **The Five of Wands**
5   **The King of Pentacles**
6   **The Ten of Cups**
7   **The Seven of Swords**
8   **The Empress**
9   **The Nine of Wands**
10   **The Eight of Wands**
11   **The Hierophant**

Interpretation

The first glance at the cards that have come up look fairly positive. Cards 1, 2 & 3 that give us a snapshot of the situation all look very romantic however take note that the crossing card is actually a very positive relationship card, the two of cups. This card in that particular position tells us that there is perhaps a fear of commitment within a relationship. If we re-examine the flow of the 'snapshot' we can see that the three of pentacles can portray someone who is very driven, perhaps a little self-focused and wants, really wants the relationship to work, the lovers in this position tells us that the relationship has promise but that the couple aren't quite on the wavelength at the moment.

The past highlighted in cards 4 & 5 tells us that there are dominant and dominating relationships in at least one of the couples background and this is a stumbling block going in to the future of the relationship portrayed by the 7th card which is the seven of swords. The seven of swords here tells us that the partners relationship history has been kept hidden and that there is a deep fear of being hurt and allowing themselves to feel vulnerable again.

There is hope though, the goal card is the ten of cups, a joyful head over heels in love feeling but the past has to be addressed and let go of in order for that to happen. If this person pushes there partner to move too quickly they will lose them. If instead they allow things to develop naturally then a very positive and loving partnership can grow and take root.

Figure 5 - The Seven Card Star Spread

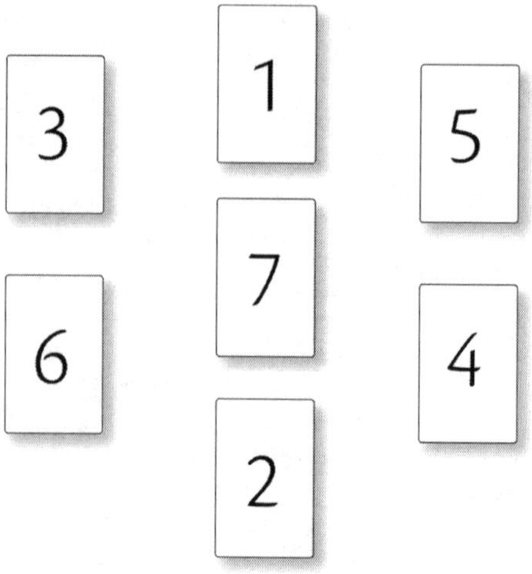

CARDS 1, 3 AND 5 - Positive reasons for doing something, positive aspects of the situation, reasons why it will work, things to focus on increasing, what is helpful in the situation

CARDS 2, 4 AND 6 - Negative aspects of the situation, reasons for not doing something, that which stands in the way and needs to be dealt with before the positive can be accessed, any unresolved issues from the past holding the client back, reasons they should not do something

CARD 7 - The core issue, the real reason, the under-lying problem, the central theme for the client, what they can learn, the deepest/highest level.

This spread is based on the symbol of the six pointed star. This consists of two triangles, one upward, the other downward. It follows the esoteric adage 'as above, so below'.

It is very good for dealing with a individual who has one issue they wish to focus on, or questions that are concerned with a 'should I/shouldn't I' scenario in terms on a relationship quandary.

Figure 6 - Sample Seven Card Star Spread

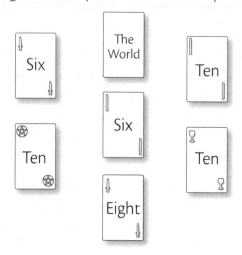

Question: My partner has suggested we make a commitment and buy a house together. Should we move in together?

1   **The World**
2   **The Eight of Swords**
3   **The Six of Swords**
4   **The Ten of Cups**
5   **The Ten of Wands**
6   **The Ten of Pentacles**
7   **The Six of Wands**

Interpretation

Well the first thing to notice here is that there are three tens within the spread indicating that this couple are at a fairly stable point and have been through quite a lot together, the World, the final card from the major Arcana is also present which again tells us that this is a couple who have a deep history and a strong connection. If we look more closely as the positive aspects of the spread relating to the question we can see that there is a strong sense of recovery and that this move would strengthen this couple and bring them closer together, the ten of wands does show us that there is a slight edge of influence from one or other family putting pressure on the couple to take this a stage further and deepen their level of commitment.

The negative aspects of the spread show us that there is a fear that they have changed too much over the years and have lost the initial spark, however this is a fear and not a reality. The presence of the ten of pentacles, normally a positive family card, shows us a warning. In this case the warning is to ensure that they don't live too close to their in-laws! The 7th card, the theme here is one of success, trust and overcoming obstacles. Go for it.

The Relationship Spread

This is by far my favorite relationship spread and is incredibly useful and informative. It can be used to gain insight and clarity on intimate relationships that you are currently involved it, you can use it retrospectively to see the reasons why a relationship didn't work and you can even use it to explore the dynamics at play between you and a work colleague or family member. Just make sure you are ready to see the truth of a situation, it isn't

Figure 7 - The Relationship Spread

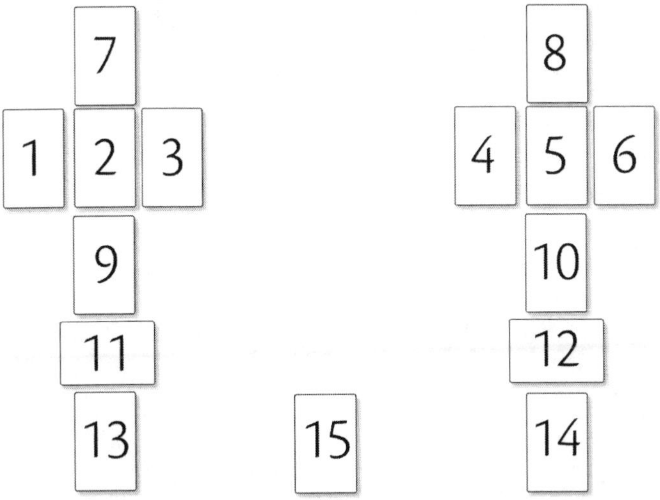

always pleasant. I once found out a partner was seeing someone else behind my back through using this spread and although I am incredibly grateful now that I found out it was very painful at the time!

CARD 1 – What she is bringing to the relationship

CARD 2 – Where she stands now, in relation to him

CARD 3 - What she is hoping to achieve or get from the relationship

CARD 4 – What he is bringing to the relationship

CARD 5 – What he is experiencing or stands within the relationship

CARD 6 – What he is hoping to achieve

CARD 7 – How she sees him

CARD 8 – How he sees her

CARD 9 – How she saw him when they first met

CARD 10 – How he saw her when they first met

CARD 11 – Her fears or unconscious anxieties

CARD 12 – His fears or unconscious anxieties

CARD 13 – External influences on her

CARD 14 – External influences on him

CARD 15 – Where the relationship will go

Figure 8 - Sample Relationship Spread

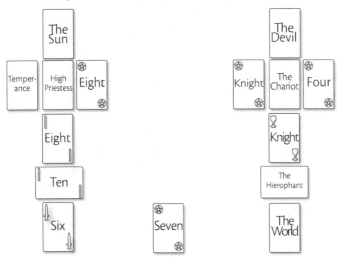

Question: what is in store for our relationship.

1   Temperance
2   The High Priestess
3   The Eight of Pentacles
4   The Knight of Pentacles
5   The Chariot
6   The Four of Pentacles
7   The Sun
8   The Devil
9   The Eight of Wands
10 The Knight of Cups
11 The Ten of Wands
12 The Hierophant
13 The Six of Swords
14 The World
15 The Seven of Pentacles

Interpretation

The spread is so enlightening because you can compare and contrast the couple as you work through it. With this particular couple we can see that they are both bringing similar things to the relationship though in very different ways, her with Temperance and the desire to bring balance, peace and stability to who she truly is and him with the Knight of pentacles which also indicates a desire for stability though through the material world and by establishing family bonds rather than in a spiritual or overly emotional way.

They both have major Arcana cards present in positions 2 and 4 in relation to how they present themselves to one another and again it is a good flow as she is the passive but strong high priestess and he is the dynamic and strong chariot bringing the changes.

We do start to see patterns of things being hidden under the surface with him and an inability to share his past or his fears about the future. She sees him as the supportive Sun but on a deeper level perhaps also she has a subconscious desire to 'fix' him comes in here or to see him as she would like him to be rather than who he actually is, that sense of wanting to 'heal' or 'fix' others is strengthened by the six of swords in her position 13 (influences upon her). He sees her as the Devil which isn't literal! It speaks of his fears and past hurts and perhaps also the fear that he himself will betray her. He desires to move forward with his life but is bogged down by old pains and commitments to others that he cannot break (we see this with Knight of wands, The Hierophant and the World) whereas she sees the version of him that he is presenting and needs to dig below that, maybe where she doesn't feel comfortable looking, to see who he really is. If she doesn't do this the road ahead is a difficult one (seven of pentacles) but there is hope, they just need to tread carefully and be very very honest. It isn't possible to scrub out the past and how someone behaved in a previous relationship. Once the past mistakes and hurts from previous relationships have been aired given a place in the open it is easier to move on.

As with all Tarot spreads, further cards can be added as appropriate. Some suggestions you may like to consider are:

The next step, How to handle this, The Final Outcome.

No Tarot spread is set in stone so follow your intuition as to what is appropriate each time you use the spread and add what cards are necessary or in response to clients' questions.

Further work on your own Relationships

I have designed a simple nine card spiral Tarot spread specifically for focusing on your own relationship patterns which you can use for your own development. It is also an excellent tool if you are already familiar with the Tarot and would like to incorporate ancestral patterns in to your work with others. The layout is illustrated below

The Root Cause
Earth Influences – message from the Pentacle Family
Air Influences – message from the Sword Family
Fire Influences – message from the Wand family
Water Influences – message from the Cup Family
Current Situation
Immediate Future
Guidance for moving forward
Final Outcome

Lay the cards out for yourself and then take a note of them all, speak aloud to yourself or scribble in to your diary your initial thoughts and emotions as you read the spread for yourself then revisit it in a few days time and interpret again what the cards are telling you. What do you need to know right now?

Designing Your Own Spread

You will soon find that you start to adapt the spreads that you are working with, adding in clarification cards and interpreting the cards in your own way. One step on from this is to design your own spread, tailored to the way in which you read tarot. This is not as difficult to do as it may sound. There are several things to consider:

The shape of your spread. At first it may be best to stick to geometrical, balanced shapes such as the square, line, circle or triangle. The first spread I designed used the infinity symbol.
Consider what it is you want to know.
What do you find useful in other spreads?
What do you find a hindrance?
Consider common themes found within spreads, such as:

Past – present – future.
Negative energies – positive energies.
External influences – Internal influences.
Dreams and ambitions.
Hopes and fears
Etc.

Be creative and have fun, you are only limited by your own imagination.

9

Working with Others

Tips to Improve Your Readings

Working with crystals can help to develop your natural intuitive abilities. You can either hold them whilst giving your reading or have them on the table beside you. I hold a piece of blue opaline when I give readings, this helps you "tune in" as well as working on your throat chakra. I also use a rainbow obsidian sphere which is traditionally used for scrying. Amethyst, rutilated amethyst, blue apatite and black opal are all excellent crystals to use to aid in divination.

To explore one part of a reading in more detail, it is very useful to use the particular card in question as a significator for a new spread. This will really help to give depth to your readings. However don't be tempted or pushed into doing this for more than a couple of cards in the spread. Some people will not be happy no matter how much information you pass on to them. Always remember that you are in control of a reading and you can and should draw the reading to a close after a certain time, say 30min. Some people become addicted to tarot readings and want to pass on responsibility for their decisions onto you. There should be at least a 3 month gap in between readings, unless they are asking about a completely unrelated area. Try to discourage your clients coming to you more often than that, it may pay the bills but you are not really helping them.

You can also substitute a negative final outcome card for a more positive card. This may seem a strange idea at first but remember when you are doing a Tarot reading you are showing someone what will happen to them if they continue on the path they are on, behaving in the same way. If they do not like what they see then they can change their behavior to alter the outcome. Explore with your individual the outcome they would like and select an appropriate card/or select one at random. Then lay down some more cards to explore how they can achieve this outcome for themselves.

It is important to always be positive when giving a reading. Obviously we all go through difficult periods in our life but the Tarot can be used to shed light on the "why" and "how" of this. A individual should always leave you feeling empowered and full of hope.

Remember to explain to your individual that a reading is accurate for the time it is given and can be accurate for 6months to a year. However nothing is set in stone, you may give them a fabulous reading telling them about new beginnings and opportunities in their life. If they do not act on this or grab these opportunities then they will most definitely pass them by. Always emphasize that they must be proactive. A Tarot reading is like a map of their life path, the individual always has the option of changing their future by changing where they are going in their present.

Sometimes you just can't connect with someone. In this case own up and say you can't read for them today, they will appreciate that a lot more than a mediocre reading.

Always be honest with your client and do not give them false hope. Remember that they will be feeling very vulnerable and exposed when sitting opposite you. Treat them with the respect and honesty they deserve, imagine always how you would feel in their position. Act with compassion and read from the heart.

Tarot Magic

Magic is the art of making coincidences happen according to your own will. Magic tends to get quite a bad press and is often associated with curses, hexes and the black arts. However people often practice forms of magic in their everyday lives without realizing it. For example lighting a candle in church and offering up a prayer is the equivalent of casting a simple spell, prayer in itself or the "mantras" you repeat to yourself in a time of need (such as "please can I get the job, please can I get the job!") are affirmations – a method of focusing your mind/will in order to align yourself with a specific energy to achieve a goal or desire. Magic need not be grand or complicated and filled with ritual. The core of practicing magic lies in your own intention and your own belief.

We have already discussed the different uses of the tarot: divination; counseling and spiritual guidance. Tarot can also be used as a link between spiritual/self development and magic. The tarot can be used as a tool to focus your energies and intentions when practicing magic. There are links with the tarot and mystical traditions such as the kabala and the order of the golden dawn, as we have discussed previously. When the tarot is used in such a way it is helping us to link in to the universal/god/spirit energy which surrounds us all. This energy is known by many names ki, qi, chi, prana to name a few. This universal energy is neutral; it is the way in which it is used that determines whether it is positive or negative in effect. It may seem obvious to state, but any magic that you practice must harm no-one and be for the greater good of ALL concerned. Do not send out intentions to harm others or act against their will. It is essential to remember that whatever energy you send out will be returned to you for good or ill. Also magic should never be your first port of call, it should instead be a last resort when all else has failed and when you are in true need, for example, it is no use casting a spell to ensure you get the job you want if you were unwilling to prepare yourself for the interview. If practicing magic for a friend remember that you will be karmically tied to them and their life path - you will be responsible for any consequences. This is not meant to sound dramatic for the sake of it. Magic when practiced correctly can be fun and a wonderful experience, but inappropriate or irresponsible magic will come back to bite you and it is a lesson once learned never forgotten, be warned!

Now if you are planning on using your tarot for magical purposes there are some guidelines to be aware of:

You should be in good physical and emotional health. You may already be aware that practicing psychic work is draining, it is for this reason that you should not consider using the tarot, in any way, if you are unwell.

If you feel drawn to tarot magic, or any other form of magic, then it is a good idea to practice regular meditation to help you focus your mind and visualize your goals.

You must ALWAYS work for the greater good.

It is a good idea to tie in any magical workings to the lunar cycle. To rid yourself of something practice your magic when the moon is waning (moving from full to new), to bring something into your life practice your magic when the moon is waxing (moving from new to full). The annual cycle can also be taken into account.

Be careful what you ask for, you might get it. Also be aware that the universe will always answer your call, however sometimes the answer will be no!

As with spread design, the pattern that you choose for you magical tarot working is very important. The cards should be placed in a harmonious and balanced pattern. To cast your own tarot magic you firstly have to pick a card(s) to reflect your aim or goal. One card should represent you, at least one card should represent your goal and there should also be a bridging card(s) showing the steps that you perceive are needed to get there. Below are some simple examples:

To find Love

Yourself: The Hermit, to represent you alone but seeking someone.

Bridging card: The Lovers Obviously representative of a couple but also wise choices & success.

Final aim: The 3 of cups. Celebration and joy at finding one another.

These is a simple example. I have not suggested anything more complicated or suggested patterns because your tarot magic will have more power and more meaning for you if you design it for yourself. It is not necessary to stick to the traditional meanings of the cards, go with what they mean to you and how you intuitively feel about them. As you are choosing the cards visualize your goal being manifested.

Once you have decided on the appropriate cards to use and the pattern that feels right to you it is time to lay out your cards in a place that you will be able to see them every day, for at least a week, without them being disturbed. It is a good idea to place them in a clip frame or something similar. As you lay out the cards offer a prayer asking for help and protection, ask that your desire be fulfilled for the greater good of all concerned. Each day spend at least five minutes meditating on the cards and repeating an affirmation of your desire in your head. You may want to light an appropriately colored candle beside your cards to help focus your mind and signal your intention to the universe. If you are unsure of what color to use white is always appropriate. Decide in advance how long you will spend focusing on your tarot magic. A week is fine for most working but use your own judgment. When you have finished dismantle your cards and offer thanks. Be patient, it may take time to receive your answer be rest assured you will have been heard.

Good Psychic hygiene

As you work with any form of energetic connection be it tarot reading, psychic work, energy healing or angelic communication you will find that you become a clearer, stronger channel the more that you work with it. You will also find that you become more sensitive to variations in the energy around you. This often begins with an awareness of the subtle changes in the way the energy around you feels.

However, your sensitivity also extends to all the other forms of energy that we encounter, and which affect us consciously or unconsciously in our daily lives, and not all of this energy is beneficial to you. For example, imagine for a moment how you feel after spending time with a friend who is feeling very depressed or negative, or after some sort of confrontation: often we are left feeling drained or 'out of sorts'. This is due to us both expending our own energy in attempting to deal with the situation, and also being affected by the energy coming from the other person. Now that you are working with energy on a more conscious level, you may experience its varying effects more strongly than you did prior to your investigation into the world of tarot. The most likely results are 'energy headaches' (usually experienced as a band of pressure round the skull, particularly over the Third Eye), nausea or feeling drained. Particularly sensitive people may experience an increase in their psychic abilities, which, although positive, can be disconcerting at first.

It is therefore important to shield yourself from any unwanted effects by maintaining a strong field of positive energy around you. There are many techniques you can use to do this, and you should get in the habit of using one every day if possible, and repeating the visualization whenever you feel the need. Here are a few suggestions:

1: Golden Bubble
This is a great visualization technique and very effective.

1. Take a moment to relax your body and focus your awareness on yourself and your breath. Breathe in and out naturally, allowing the breath to flow. As you inhale, imagine you are breathing in pure light, as you exhale, release any tension and stress.

2. Focus now on your connection to this pure energy. Feel the pure white light entering your Crown chakra, flowing down your energy channel and filling your abdomen. As you breathe in, feel the energy swell within you, and as you breathe out, allow it to radiate out from your abdomen, gradually spreading over your whole body and out into your aura. Remember that the energy is limitless: as you spread it out, more and more energy floods in to fill you.

3. Allow the energy to form a ball or bubble of pure golden light, surrounding and protecting you. This bubble allows free passage of positive energy, both to and from you, but disperses and transforms any negativity you may encounter. Spend some time visualizing yourself inside your energy bubble, and keep an awareness of it with you throughout the day. When you find yourself in a negative environment, bring your awareness back to your bubble and to your connection with the energy or white light: send white light out towards the situation, and allow your golden bubble to disperse any negativity coming towards you.

2. Guides & Angels

If you feel comfortable with the concept of guides and angels, or have had direct experience of their help and protection, you may wish to ask for their presence and assistance, either on a daily basis, or at moments when you feel the need. You may ask for the help of any being you feel drawn to work with, either your own guide or guardian angel or energies such as Archangel Michael (Angel of Protection), or Goddess energy or Christ energy. It is often a good idea to ask for their presence by using their name 3 times – this is a powerful invocation, and prevents negative interference. Always remember to acknowledge and thank them for their help.

3.Closing Down and Grounding

Closing Down

After meditation or psychic work, your chakras, particularly the Crown and Third Eye, will be much more open and energized than usual. It is advisable to spend some time re-balancing and closing these chakras down before going back out into the 'real world', as you may feel a little spaced out or vulnerable, and can attract negative energy.

Spend a moment relaxing and focusing your awareness on your physical body. Allow your breath to flow naturally and quietly observe the sensations in your own body.

Focus on your feet, feel the surface upon which you stand. Visualize roots growing out of the centre of the soles of your feet. Feel these roots burrowing through the floor upon which you are standing, through the foundations of the building, down into the earth. Imagine the roots growing deeper and deeper until they reach the centre of the earth. Feel yourself connected to the earth through your feet.

Now visualize your Crown chakra as a white flower, perhaps a lotus or a rose, above your head. The flower is in full bloom, the petals wide open.

Now begin to gently close over the petals of the flower in your mind. Do not close the flower over completely, just allow it to softly close in on itself until it is a lightly-furled bud again, still giving and receiving energy, but in a gentle, relaxing flow.

Repeat the process with any other chakra you feel needs attention (it is usually a good idea to close the Third Eye down a little after energy work). For each chakra, visualize a flower of the appropriate color, or if you prefer, just imagine a glowing, spinning light in each energy centre, and adjust the size and intensity of the light.

You may sense that some chakras are already quite restricted, and if need be, you can visualize them opening up, receiving energy from above until they are in balance with the others. Adjust the size of the flower/ the brightness of the light for all the energy centers, until you feel balanced, grounded, and energized.

Slowly bring your awareness back to your body, to your surroundings, wiggle your fingers and toes, and open your eyes gently.

Grounding
If you feel light-headed, groggy or 'spaced' after psychic work, there are a few things you can do to ground yourself again:

Send energy to your feet
Have a warm drink and/or a light snack – something sweet is
    good
If you feel queasy, or can feel a lot of energy moving about, sit

down with your hands flat on your thighs for a few minutes until the energy settles

Other tips for good 'psychic hygiene':

Cleanse your home and any space you use for energy work on a regular basis: you can do this using a sage 'smudge stick' (white sage smells nicest) or burning incense in each corner of the room, your chair, and anywhere else you feel drawn to. You can use the Golden Bubble over your reading area as well.

You can use crystals for protection, either for yourself, or placed around your home. Black and red crystals are particularly effective, e.g. black tourmaline and red jasper. Place them above doors and windows and in corners, and link them together energetically to form a protective 'grid'.

Above all be mindful of your own energy and your energetic space when you work with the tarot and ensure that you work from a place of integrity whether you are reading for yourself or for someone else.

Dodona Books offers a broad spectrum of divination systems to suit all, including Astrology, Tarot, Runes, Ogham, Palmistry, Dream Interpretation, Scrying, Dowsing, I Ching, Numerology, Angels and Faeries, Tasseomancy and Introspection.